For Tracus:

" Happy cooking "

Suzette Lord Weldon

Suzette's
International
Cooking

Review

Here's a cookbook for working folks who want to serve delicious dinners without spending all day in the kitchen. When your guests exclaim, "How did you do all this?" just smile and say, "I have a wonderful friend named Suzette."

Margie Bauman
Alaska Journal of Commerce

Suzette's International Cooking

Suzette Lord Weldon

NORTHBOOKS
Eagle River, Alaska

Art Credits: Mike Schnieble and Jim Weldon—cover design
                  Lisa Redington—chapter art

Photo Credits: Front cover globe: National Aeronautics and Space Agency
                                                          www.nasa.gov
                  Personal collection of author

Published by:

ꞐORꞆꞕBOOKS
17050 N. Eagle River Loop Road, # 3
Eagle River, Alaska 99577
www.northbooks.com

Printed in the United States of America

ISBN 978-0-9789766-3-7

Library of Congress Control Number: 2007903023

iv

Dedication

To my husband John, my hero.

Contents

Chapter 4—Chef Suzette's Italian Favorites

Chapter 5—Chef Suzette's Chinese Favorites

Chapter 6—Chef Suzette's Favorites From India

Chapter 7—Chef Suzette's Philippine Favorites

Foreword

Often, we find that the friends we are drawn to have crossed our paths in the past. This is the case with Suzette Lord Weldon and myself. It seemed so strange to come all the way to Alaska, only to reacquaint with a fine professional I'd encountered in the wine country of California several decades earlier.

Time allows all of us to grow, but I believe Suzette must have been born fully mature! She has always been far more mature than her age while maintaining a wide-eyed innocence about the world around her. The fascination she may display toward strangers is not calculated, but a genuine interest. Her skill at retaining information has served her and her public very well.

Although she is always "The Chef" in all she creates, Suzette has a flair and a grace about her that is like no other. The recipes and the presentation of her creations give the term "distinguished" an all-new meaning and comfort. She attends both her uniquely tasty dishes and the clientele/consumer with consummate knowledge and endearment.

As you stroll through her recipes, know that you are in good hands. The beauty Suzette shares in this cookbook is truly larger than life. Although she has catered many events for us with the thought in mind of healthy, colorful and unique foods, Suzette has also captured the hearts of those she served, including my own boss, Bishop MacDonald. She has designed and presented her creations at ordinations, press conferences, and other vital functions for both the Episcopal Diocese of Alaska and our program, the Beacons of Hope.

Eat well, eat wisely, eat enjoyably.

> The Rev. Patricia S. Ortiz, Director
> Beacons of Hope Ministry
> Episcopal Diocese of Alaska

Preface

Nowadays, any would-be cook can find recipes for anything on the Internet, but the question is, just how good are they?

In *Suzette's International Cooking*, you will find the best proven and delicious recipes for classic traditional dishes from seven nations.

Some are very true to their origins, and some I have tweaked just enough to be more pleasing to more palates. Such is the case with my dolmades. The more traditionally-made dolmades just didn't appeal to some of my clients, so a little change here and there, and twenty years later we are still enjoying this very special recipe, a favorite and much-in-demand dish.

Ever since I was a little girl, my life has centered around love, laughter, and good food. I was raised in the San Francisco Bay Area of California, where great food from all over the world was a mainstay in many homes and restaurants. And, oh, did my mother and I love and take advantage of the abundance of great cuisine! We tasted, critiqued, and studied many delicious foods from around the world.

My mother could replicate anything she tasted. She would find the best of the best, and then figure out how it was prepared. My children and I still carry on this tradition.

In the following pages, you will find my favorite recipes that have been thus perfected. I have been using these recipes for many years in my catering businesses, and have taught many of my students in cooking classes to prepare them. Now I've decided to share my most favorite and, up until now, secret recipes in a series of cookbooks, starting with my international favorites.

I hope you enjoy this book, with my blessings.

–Suzette Lord Weldon

Acknowledgments

Special thanks to Jim Weldon and Alice Wittig for the time spent editing, proofreading, and typesetting my cookbook and making this project possible. And a special thank you to Mike Schnieble for his finishing touches on our cover design.

Thanks also to my daughter Desiree for all her hard work tasting, typing, and being my best all-around helper, and to my son Bob for being a great taster and ready to muscle a load around.

Thanks to my students, whose enthusiasm and appreciation fueled my aspiration to do these cookbooks.

To my publishers, Ray and Jan Holmsen of Northbooks, who were so fantastic to work with that I'm already starting on my next cookbook.

I am indebted as well to all my family and friends who encouraged me and had faith in my talents and skills.

And last but not least, my mother, Lourdes, who is a kitchen genius.

One cannot think well,
love well, sleep well
if one has not dined well
—Virginia Woolf

Chapter 1
Chef Suzette's

Mexican
Favorites

©Lisa Redington

Salsa (sahl-sah)

Real simple; real good!

Basic Salsa Ingredients:

4 large tomatoes, diced (preferably home grown)
1 small onion, diced
1 jalapeno, minced fine
¼ cup cilantro leaves, washed and chopped up
dash of salt
3 teaspoons of Tapatio hot sauce*

Preparation:

Mix all together and chill for at least an hour to allow flavors to blend.

To make fruit salsas:

Substitute fruit for tomatoes, such as
blueberries
mangos
pineapple
etc.

———

* Available in most supermarkets.

Guacamole (gwah-kah-moh-lee)

I like my guacamole simple; too many ingredients and I think it takes away from the avocado's delicate flavor.

Ingredients:

3 large avocados
1 tablespoon lemon juice
3 tablespoons onion, minced
1 tablespoon garlic, minced
1 teaspoon Tabasco sauce
½ teaspoon Worcestershire sauce
salt and pepper

Preparation:

Mash avocados with masher or fork. Add lemon juice, onion, garlic, Tabasco sauce, Worcestershire sauce, salt and pepper to taste.

Arroz a la Mexicana (ah-rohs; Spanish Rice)

Once you learn this recipe, it gets easier every time you make it.

Ingredients:

1½ cups long grain white rice
hot water
3 tablespoons peanut or vegetable oil
1 large tomato
⅓ medium onion
1 garlic clove, peeled
3½ cups well-salted chicken broth
½ cup carrots, minced small (pea size)
⅓ cup peas

Preparation:

In large sauce pan, pour enough hot water over the rice to cover it. Let stand for 15 minutes. Drain and rinse under cold water. Shake and drain.

Shake the rice one more time to rid it of any excess water and stir it into the oil in a 12-inch frying pan with at least 1½- to 2-inch sides. Coat the grains well. Fry until the grains are a pale gold color (approximately 10 minutes).

In a blender, blend the tomato with the onion and garlic to a smooth puree. Add this to the rice and cook over a high flame, stirring constantly until it is almost dry.

Stir in the broth and vegetables into the rice. Cook over medium heat uncovered until most of the liquid has been absorbed. Cover the pan and allow to cook over a low flame for 5 minutes. Remove from heat and set aside, still covered, and allow to steam itself for 30 minutes.

4

Black Beans

My students are always surprised by how flavorful these beans turn out.

Ingredients:

2 cups dried black beans, washed
½ small onion, minced, or 2 shallots, minced
3 cups chicken broth

Preparation:

In large sauce pan, add twice as much water as black beans. Bring to a boil. Turn the heat off, cover and let soak for one hour.

Drain the beans after they have soaked. Return to the pot and add the broth and onions. Bring to a boil and keep at a boil for 15-20 minutes. Simmer until tender.

Tamale Dough (tuh-mah-lee)

One year I had four classes scheduled for January and February, and I ended up teaching eight classes. Everyone, it seems, wanted to learn to make tamales.

Ingredients:

2 cups Maseca* for tamales
2 cups lukewarm water or broth
1 teaspoon baking powder
½ teaspoon salt
⅔ cup vegetable shortening

Preparation:

Combine the masa, baking powder and salt in a bowl. Work in the water/broth using your fingers until a soft dough forms. In a small mixing bowl, whip the shortening until fluffy. Add to the masa and beat until the dough forms a spongy texture.

Prepare the tamales with desired filling.

Yield: 16 small tamales

———

*Maseca Instant Corn Masa Mix is a product from Azteca Milling, available at most supermarkets.

Making Tamales

1. Corn husks- Purchased corn husks will be dry. To soften them for use, pour very hot water over them and let them soak for 30 minutes. Shake them well to rid them of excess water and pat dry.

2. Assembling- Smear a thin coating of the tamale dough over the broadest part of the husk, allowing for turning down about 1½ inches at the bottom broad part of the leaf and about 3 inches at the pointed top. Spread the chicken molé down the middle of the dough (for chicken molé recipe, see following page). Overlap the sides of the husks loosely to allow the dough to expand. Turn up the pointed end of the leaf and fold the broader end over it. Tear some of the husks lengthwise into narrow strips and use one for tying each tamale across the flap.

3. Cooking- Fill the bottom of a steamer with water up to the level indicated and bring to a boil. Line the top of the steamer with corn husks, covering the bottom and sides. Stack the tamales upright. For best results, do not over pack, but pack in firmly. Cover tightly and allow to steam for 2½ hours over a medium flame. Keep the water simmering, not boiling. To test for doneness, remove one from the center and one from the side and gently open them. The dough should be cooked throughout.

Chicken Molé (moh-lay)

Ingredients:

1½-pound chicken
2 tablespoons oil
1 medium onion, -minced
2 tablespoons flour
1½ cups chicken broth
4 tablespoons molé sauce*

Preparation:

Cook the chicken until tender. Shred or chop chicken into small pieces and set aside.

In a sauce pan, heat the oil and sauté the onion until translucent. Add the flour and the chicken and cook for two minutes. Add the chicken broth and molé sauce. Combine well and simmer for 1 hour.

Add a bit more broth if it's too dry. You want some sauce, but not soupy.

———

*Several choices of brands can be found at your local market.

Carne Asada (kahr-nay ah-sah-dah)

Carne asada is great in tacos, burritos, or taquitos.

Ingredients:

2 pounds beef roast (rump, tri-tip, or almost any similar cut)
¾ cup lime juice
4-6 cloves garlic

Preparation:

To prepare the beef, combine the juice, garlic and beef, place in a plastic bag, and allow to marinate overnight or up to 24 hours. (Rule of thumb: the more tender the cut, the less it has to marinate. The tougher the cut, the longer it needs to marinate.) Heat a grill or grill pan over a medium high heat. Cook the beef until desired doneness. Slice and enjoy!

Serving suggestions:

For burritos: Serve with Spanish rice, flour tortillas, black beans, guacamole, salsa, and sour cream.

For tacos: Serve with flour or corn tortilla shells, grilled green onions, whole jalapenos, radishes, and lime wedges.

For taquitos: Roll up in corn tortillas and fry. Serve with guacamole and salsas.

Chili Relleno (chee-lee reh-yeh-noh)

This is the best chili relleno recipe I've made. I use homegrown yellow tomatoes for the broth, and it looks beautiful that way.

Ingredients:

for the chilies:

8 poblano chilies
cheese
flour
4 eggs, separated
¼ teaspoon salt

for the tomato broth:

1¼ pounds tomatoes, peeled and seeded
1 medium onion
2 cloves garlic, chopped
vegetable oil for frying

Preparation:

Prepare the tomato broth by blending the ingredients together.

To prepare the chilies, fire roast fast on a gas range or grill till black all over but not cooked through. As each is done, put into a slightly wet towel to steam, then scrape off burned area with edge of knife, slice the top off and gently scoop out seeds. Stuff with cheese and roll in flour.

To prepare the batter, whip the egg whites until stiff. Add the salt and yolks one by one, beating well after each addition.

Dip the chilies in the batter and fry in a frying pan in about ⅛ inch of oil until golden brown. Drain on a towel.

Serving suggestion:

Place the tomato broth on a plate and top with a relleno for a beautiful presentation.

Chili Verde (chee-lee vehr-deh)

When I make chili verde I have to make it extra hot so that I can't eat too much. I love this recipe.

Ingredients:

flour tortillas
2 pounds boneless pork, lean and tender, not too fatty
1 large onion, diced small
5-10 cloves garlic
tomatillos*
½ bunch cilantro, washed and chopped
2 or 3 Jalapenos, or to taste
vegetable oil

Preparation:

Cut pork into ½ inch pieces. In 3-quart sauce pan, add the oil to the cool pan. Heat the pan over a medium heat and add the pork. Brown on all sides. Then *(This is very important!)* remove excess oil from pan.

Peel and wash the tomatillos. Cut into small pieces and place in a blender with a small amount of water, about ⅛ cup. Add jalapenos. Blend until smooth. Pour into the pan with the pork, stirring to deglaze the pan. Add the remaining ingredients and simmer for about 45 minutes.

———

*If you can't find tomatillos, read the ingredient list on a can of salsa verde to make sure they are using tomatillos in their sauce, and you can substitute with it.

Notes

Chapter 2
Chef Suzette's
Greek
(Middle Eastern)
Favorites

©Lisa Redington

Dolma; pl. Dolmades: Stuffed Grape Leaves

(Dohl-mah-dehs)

I've been making these for 25 years. Be careful; they're addictive!

Ingredients:

1 jar grape leaves, drained and rinsed (lay on towel to dry) – Also cut off the tough parts of the stems.
¾ pound ground lamb or hamburger
4 cups cooked long grain rice
½ cup pine nuts
2 shallots, minced
juice of 1½ lemons
½ cup butter
1 tablespoon fresh parsley, minced
1 teaspoon fresh mint, minced (optional)

Preparation:

In sauce pan, cook the ground lamb. Near the end of the browning process, add shallots. Drain and cool. Mix cooked lamb, cooked rice, and pine nuts and parsley. Lay each grape leaf flat with stem end toward you. Put about 1 tablespoon of filling on it, or more if the leaf is large. Fold both sides in, then roll up from the stem end. In large frying pan, melt butter. When just melted, add lemon juice, then carefully lay the stuffed grape leaves in the pan, seam side down. Turn over carefully and cook just until leaves are translucent on all sides.

Hummus (Hoom-uhs)

*Healthy and delicious. I do some pretty unusual things with hummus.**

Ingredients:

1 can garbanzo beans, drained
$^1/_8$ cup tahini (Sesame Paste)†
4-6 cloves garlic, chopped
1 lemon, juiced
$^1/_3$ cup olive oil
salt and pepper to taste
pinch of cayenne pepper

Preparation:

Place garbanzos, garlic and tahini in a large blender. Blend well. Add olive oil in a stream and blend to a creamy consistency. Add salt, pepper, cayenne, and lemon juice and blend for another minute. If your hummus is thick and has a dry consistency, add water in about $^1/_8$ cup amounts and blend until the desired consistency is achieved. It should be almost like a soft, creamy peanut butter.

Set the hummus in a serving bowl.

You can eat it right away, but it will improve if left to sit overnight in refrigerator.

Garnish with branches of parsley and sprinkle with paprika or cayenne. Serve with toasted pita bread wedges. It makes a wonderful dip for raw veggies, tortilla and corn chips, and is great for tortilla wraps as well!

———

*See in upcoming volumes of my cookbook.

†Available in most markets.

Greek Salad

It's best when made with homegrown tomatoes and a really good extra virgin olive oil.

Ingredients:

3 large ripe tomatoes
1 English cucumber
1 small red onion
1 small jar kalamata olives
1 6- to 8-ounce package feta cheese (flavored version optional), crumbled
½ cup olive oil
1 to 2 tablespoons lemon juice

Preparation:

Cut tomatoes into wedges.
Cut onions into 1½-inch pieces.
Slice cucumber ¼ inch thick and then in half.
Then toss all ingredients together.
Chill in refrigerator until serving time.

Serving suggestions:

Serve on a bed of butter leaf lettuce.

Gyros (Jeer-oh; Zheer-oh; Yeer-oh)

A Greek specialty consisting of spiced lamb that is usually molded around a spit and vertically roasted. But patties are more practical to make at home.

Ingredients:

½ cup minced onion
1 clove garlic, minced
½ pound ground lamb
2 tablespoons lemon juice
½ teaspoon dried oregano
½ teaspoon ground cumin
½ cup seeded, peeled cucumber, grated
¼ cup non-fat yogurt
1 tablespoon fresh mint, chopped (optional)
2 pitas
½ cup shredded lettuce
½ cup diced tomato

Preparation:

Spray skillet with no-stick spray. Add onions and garlic and cook until soft, stirring constantly.

Place in mixing bowl with lamb, lemon juice, oregano and cumin, and mix thoroughly. Shape into 2 patties.

Place on rack of broiler and broil for 3-4 minutes on each side, turning once, or until desired doneness is reached.

Combine cucumber, yogurt and mint in small bowl and mix.

Cut around the edge of each pita bread and pull open to form a pocket. Fill each pita with half of the lettuce and tomato, 1 lamb patty, and half the yogurt mixture.

Souvlaki (soo vlah-kee)

Not as well known as Gyros but just as good.

Ingredients:

2 pounds tender boneless pork, cut into 1-inch squares
½ cup extra virgin olive oil
1 tablespoon fresh grated garlic
⅓ cup lemon juice

Preparation:

1. Mix olive oil, garlic, and lemon juice.

2. Marinate pork in mixture overnight

3. Place marinated pork on skewers (metal or presoaked bamboo)

4. Grill indoor on cast-iron grill pan or outdoors.

5. Serve with pita bread and Tzatziki (dzah-dzee-kee) sauce, and slices of tomato, cucumber, and red onion.

Tzatziki (dzah-dzee-kee)

Tzatziki can be served as a dip, cracker spread or condiment for dishes such as Gyros and Souvlaki.

Ingredients:

1 8-ounce plain yogurt
1 whole cucumber, seeds removed and grated
½ teaspoon minced garlic or to taste
Optional: minced dill or mint/splash olive oil or vinegar

Preparation:

1. Mix all together.

Spanakopitas (Spahn-uh-koh-pih-tuh)

These tasty little packages are fun to make and popular, so when you make them, make a lot.

Ingredients:

2 tablespoons olive oil
1 small onion, diced
1 10-ounce package frozen minced spinach, thawed and squeezed dry.
1 egg
½ cup grated parmesan cheese
8 ounces feta cheese, crumbled
⅛ teaspoon pepper
about ⅓ pound phyllo dough (strudel leaves)
½ cup butter

Preparation:

1. In 2-quart saucepan over medium heat, in hot oil, cook onion until tender. Remove from heat; stir in spinach, egg, cheeses, and pepper.

2. With knife, cut phyllo lengthwise into 2-inch wide strips. Place strips on waxed paper and cover with damp towel.

3. Brush top of one strip of phyllo with melted butter; place 1 teaspoonful of mixture at short end of strip.

4. Fold one corner of strip diagonally over filling so the short end forms a right triangle.

5. Continue folding over at each end of strip to form a triangular-shaped package.

6. Preheat oven to 350°F. Place packages, seam side down, in 15½ by 10½ inch baking pan; brush with butter. Bake triangles 15 minutes or until golden brown. Serve hot.

Moussaka (moo-sah-kah)

It's like a savory eggplant casserole. I use moosemeat for what I then call Moose-saka. It works great–if you have moose!

Ingredients:

3 medium-sized eggplant, peeled
1 cup onions, finely chopped
¾ cup olive oil or butter
2 pounds lean ground lamb
1 cup canned or fresh diced tomatoes, drained
3 tablespoons tomato paste
⅓ cup white wine or chicken stock
¼ teaspoon nutmeg
a grating of black pepper
3 egg whites
½ cup fine bread crumbs
3 eggs, yolks beaten
grated parmesan cheese
2 tablespoons fresh parsley, chopped

Preparation:

1. Peel and slice eggplant and let drain in a colander at least 45 minutes.

2. Meanwhile, sauté onions in ¼ cup olive oil or butter until golden.

3. Add ground lamb. Cook until brown, then add tomatoes, tomato paste, chopped parsley, white wine/stock, nutmeg and black pepper. Simmer the mixture about 45 minutes.

4. On the side, quickly sauté the drained eggplant on all sides in ½ cup olive oil or butter, using only a little oil at a time, since eggplant soaks it up. Drain on paper towel.

5. Beat egg whites until stiff but not dry, fold into cooked, cooled meat mixture. Then fold in fine bread crumbs.

6. Prepare a double portion of white sauce.* When hot, pour a small amount of sauce into 3 beaten egg yolks and a grating of nutmeg to temper the eggs. Then pour mixture into the rest of the white sauce.

7. Preheat oven to 350°F. Assemble the ingredients in a 9 x 13-inch or larger baking dish, placing first a layer of eggplant, then the meat mixture, and ending with an eggplant layer. Cover the whole with sauce. Sprinkle the top generously with grated parmesan cheese. Bake the casserole until thoroughly heated through, but do not allow the mixture to reach the boiling point.

The moussaka can be cut into squares if you will allow it to stand about 20 minutes before serving.

———

*White sauce below.

White Sauce

Simply basic white sauce

Ingredients:

3 tablespoons butter
3 tablespoons flour
1 cup milk
pinch nutmeg

Preparation:

1. Melt butter over low heat.
2. Blend flour into melted butter, stirring constantly for 1 to 3 minutes with a whisk. Remove from heat.
3. Whisk milk and nutmeg into cooled flour and butter mixture.
4. Return to low heat, stirring constantly, about 3 minutes, until the sauce thickens.

Baba Ghanoush (bah-bah-gah-noosh)

Creamed eggplant with tahini dip. Also great for tortilla wraps, pita (pee-tah) bread, or lavosh (lah-vohsh), a round, thin, crisp or soft, popular middle eastern flat bread.

Ingredients:

1 medium eggplant
3 cloves of garlic, peeled
4 tablespoons tahini (sesame seed paste)*
3 to 4 tablespoons lemon juice
salt to taste

Preparation:

Preheat the broiler

Prick the eggplant with a fork and place in a foil lined pan and set in broiler. When skin gets charred on one side, turn the eggplant a quarter turn. Keep turning till the whole eggplant is charred. Peel away charred skin and rinse quickly, then pat dry.

In a food processor combine garlic, eggplant, tahini, lemon juice, and salt, and blend until smooth. Serve at room temperature or cold with pita bread.

———

* found in specialty markets.

Falafel (fuh-lah-fehl)

Usually small, deep-fried patties or balls made of highly seasoned ground chickpeas (garbanzo beans).

Ingredients:

1 can chickpeas (garbanzos)
1 teaspoon baking soda
1 teaspoon salt
½ cup very finely minced onion
2 tablespoons very finely minced parsley
1 teaspoon ground roasted cumin seeds
1 teaspoon ground coriander
2 cloves garlic, peeled and mashed to a pulp
a little freshly ground black pepper
1 tablespoon lemon juice
⅛ teaspoon cayenne pepper
oil for deep frying

Preparation:

Place chickpeas in a food processor. Add baking soda and salt. Blend till you have the texture of coarse bread crumbs. Empty chickpeas into a bowl. Add onion, parsley, cumin, coriander, garlic, black pepper, lemon juice, and cayenne. Mix gently with a fork. The mixture should be loose and crumbly.

Put 2 inches of oil in a wok or other utensil for deep frying and set to heat on a medium low heat. While oil heats form batter into patties using a light touch. Make patties 2 inches in diameter and ¾ inch thick. Fry about 4 minutes or until reddish-brown on each side, then remove and drain on paper towel.

Serve hot with tahini dipping sauce. Or make a sandwich with pita bread with sliced cucumber, sliced tomatoes, a shot or two of hot sauce and of course tahini sauce. (Recipe overleaf.)

Tahini Dipping Sauce (tah-hee-nee)

Ingredients:

3 cloves garlic, peeled
¼ cup tahini (sesame paste)*
4 tablespoons lemon juice
 ¼ to ½ teaspoon salt
3 tablespoons cold water

Preparation:

Crush the garlic cloves to a paste. Place paste in a food processor.
Add the tahini and beat it in. Add lemon juice and salt and beat in
the same as before. Add cold water, a little bit at a time, beating in as
well.

———

* found in specialty markets.

Stuffed Peaches with Mascarpone

(mahs-cahr-poh-nee)

Mascarpone is a buttery-rich double- or triple-cream cheese made from cow's milk. This delicately flavored cheese is very versatile. Try in place of cream cheese in some recipes for a change.

Ingredients:

4 large peaches, halved and pitted or 8 canned peach halves
1½ ounces amoretto cookies, crumbled
2 tablespoons almonds, ground
3 tablespoons sugar
1 tablespoon cocoa powder
⅔ cup sweet wine (Marsala)
2 tablespoons butter
mascarpone

Preparation:

Preheat oven to 400°F. Combine the amoretti, ground almonds, sugar, and cocoa. Add enough wine to make the mixture into a thick paste. Place the peaches in a buttered ovenproof dish and fill them with the stuffing. Dot with butter and pour remaining wine into the dish. Bake for 35 minutes at 375°F. Remove the peaches from the oven and let them cool. Serve at room temperature with the mascarpone.

Baklava (Bahk-lah-vah)

This recipe is not as heavy as others. The apricot nectar brightens it up nicely.

Ingredients:

1 pound phyllo dough
½ pound sweet butter
2 cups ground walnuts or pistachios

Preparation:

Preheat oven to 275°F.

Grease an 11 x 16-inch baking pan. Melt butter, lay one sheet of phyllo on bottom of pan, and brush with the butter. (If it doesn't exactly fit, fold the edges over to make it fit the pan.) Repeat until you have used approximately half the sheets.

Spread nuts evenly over the entire surface.

Continue layering sheets of phyllo on top of the nut layer.

Pour any remaining butter over the top.

Cut into diagonal strips to form diamond shapes.

Bake for 1½ hours (Watch it carefully after 1 hour to make sure it doesn't get overdone. The top should be a light golden brown.)

Syrup Ingredients:

3 cups sugar
2 cups apricot nectar
2 tablespoons honey
1 tablespoon lemon juice

Preparation:

Bring all the ingredients to the boil. Reduce heat and simmer to a heavy syrup (approximately 20-25 minutes).

When bakalava comes out of oven, brush surface lightly with butter, then pour the warm syrup over the pastry, a little at a time, until all is absorbed. Allow to cool for several hours.

Makes approximately 30 diamonds.

Baklava freezes very successfully.

Notes

Chapter 3

Chef Suzette's

French
Favorites

Tapenade (ta-pen-ahd)

This spread is great on crackers, crostini or crudites, or use a little as a flavor booster for sauces or fish cakes.

Ingredients:

1½ cups pitted black or pitted kalamata olives
2-ounce can anchovy fillets, drained
2 tablespoons capers
½ cup olive oil
zest of 1 lemon
pinch of ground black pepper

Preparation:

To prepare the tapenade, finely chop the olives, anchovies, and capers. Beat these three ingredients together with the oil, lemon zest, and pepper.

Lasts for approximately one week in refrigerator.

French Onion Soup

A lot easier to make then most people think, and a great way to use the summer onions.

Ingredients:

1½ cups onions, thinly sliced
3 tablespoons butter
6 cups beef both
¼ teaspoon freshly-ground black pepper
½ teaspoon dry sherry per individual casserole dish
French bread
mozzarella cheese.

Preparation:

1. Sauté onions in butter until golden brown.

2. Add broth and ground pepper, cover; cook over low heat 30 minutes. Now put the soup into individual casserole dishes and add dry sherry.

3. Cover with sliced toasted French bread with a slice of mozzarella cheese melted on top.

Vichyssoise (vihsh-ee-swahz)

A rich creamy potato and leek soup that's usually served cold. I, myself, prefer it better hot. Sometimes I add a little crumbled pancetta to add a new dimension to the flavor.

Ingredients:

2 tablespoons butter
1 cup chopped leeks, white part and also the lighter green part, chopped very thin.
½ teaspoon powdered chicken bouillon or 1 cube
⅔ cup water
3 large potatoes, boiled till tender and mashed but left slightly lumpy
1 cup half & half
½ cup milk

Preparation:

1. In 10-inch skillet over medium heat, in hot butter, cook leeks 5 minutes; add chicken bouillon and water. Heat to boiling. Reduce heat to low; cover and simmer.

2. Add potatoes, half and half, and milk. Cook 3 minutes or until hot. Serve chilled or hot.

Ratatouille (ra-tuh-too-ee)

This is a standard summer dish for us. Using all fresh garden vegetables, it's the best. Use as main course, side dish or condiment.

Ingredients:

½ cup olive or salad oil
1 large onion, diced
3-4 large garlic cloves, minced
1 medium eggplant, cut in 1-inch chunks
1 medium red and 1 medium yellow bell pepper, cut in 1-inch pieces
3 medium zucchini, cut in 1-inch thick slices
½ cup water
1 tablespoon salt
2 tablespoons oregano leaves
2 large tomatoes, cut in wedges

Preparation:

1. In 6-quart Dutch oven or saucepot over medium heat, in hot olive oil, cook onion and garlic until tender, about 10 minutes, stirring occasionally.

2. Add eggplant and bell peppers; cook for 5 minutes, stirring mixture frequently.

3. Stir in zucchini, water, salt, and oregano; heat to boiling. Reduce heat to medium low; cook 30 minutes until vegetables are tender, stirring occasionally.

4. Stir in tomato wedges and heat through; serve hot or follow step 5

5. Cover vegetables mixture and refrigerate to serve cold later.

Coq au Vin (kohk oh vahn)

This classic French dish is composed of pieces of chicken, mushrooms, onions, bacon, and various herbs, cooked together with red wine.

Ingredients:

4 strips of bacon
1 3- to 3½-pound chicken, cut up
½ pound small mushrooms
1 medium onion, diced
¼ cup shallots, minced
1 garlic clove, minced
1 cup good dry red wine
¾ cup water
½ teaspoon thyme leaves
1 bay leaf
4 parsley sprigs
2 tablespoons butter, softened
2 tablespoons all-purpose flour

Preparation:

1. In 8-quart Dutch oven over medium heat, cook 4 strips bacon until crisp, stirring often. With slotted spoon, remove bacon to paper towels to drain. In drippings, cook chicken until browned, about 20 minutes. Remove to medium bowl.

2. Spoon off all but about ⅛ cup fat from Dutch oven; add mushrooms, onions, shallots and garlic. Cook until just wilted, about 5 minutes, stirring occasionally. Stir in wine, water, thyme, pepper, bay leaves, and parsley. Place chicken and bacon over vegetables. Over high heat, heat to boiling. Reduce heat to low; cover; simmer 20 minutes or until chicken is fork tender.

3. Meanwhile, in a cup, blend butter and flour.

4. Remove chicken and vegetables to platter; discard bay leaf and parsley. Blend flour mixture into pan juices. Heat to boiling, stirring. Spoon over chicken.

Dijon Chicken (dee-john)

Chicken roasts about 20 minutes a pound.
This dish is one of my children's favorite. They now make it
themselves.

Ingredients:

2½- to 3-pound chicken
¾ cup Dijon mustard
chicken broth
or
2 teaspoons powdered chicken bullion or 2 cubes
½ teaspoon white pepper

Preparation:

1. Roast a good-size chicken till about ¾ of the way done.

2. Pour off drippings into measuring cup, pour off fat, leaving the broth. Add more broth, or add water to make 2 cups and to this add chicken bullion. Add white pepper. Stir in Dijon mustard.

3. Pour over and around chicken, then cook till done.

Serving suggestions:

Serve over rice, with mashed potatoes, or with roasted potatoes.

Coquilles St. Jacques (Koh-keel sahn-zhahk)

This is my favorite scallop recipe.

Ingredients:

1 pound fresh or thawed frozen scallops
½ cup water
4 tablespoons dry sherry
½ teaspoon salt
⅛ teaspoon cayenne pepper
3 tablespoons butter or margarine
½ pound mushrooms, sliced
1 small onion, minced
½ garlic clove, minced
1 tablespoon chopped fresh parsley
¼ cup all-purpose flour
¾ cup buttered crumbs (See following page.)
2 tablespoons grated parmesan cheese

Preparation:

1. In 10-inch skillet over high heat, heat to boiling scallops, water, wine, salt and cayenne pepper. Reduce heat to medium; simmer scallops 2 minutes or until tender.

2. Drain scallops, reserving liquid; set aside. Grease 8 scallops shells or souffle dishes. Meanwhile, preheat oven to 400°F.

3. In same skillet over medium heat, in hot butter cook mushrooms and onion 5 minutes or until tender. Stir in garlic, parsley and flour.

4. Gradually stir in reserved liquid and cook, stirring constantly, until mixture is thickened.

5. Add the cooked scallops to skillet and stir them into hot thickened mixture.

6. Carefully spoon the scallop mixture into greased scallop shells* or souffle dishes. Then place them on baking sheet.

7. Sprinkle scallop mixture with butter crumbs and cheese and bake 10 minutes or until crumbs are golden. Serve immediately.

———————

* found in specialty cooking stores.

Butter Crumbs

Ingredients:

½ cup fresh bread crumbs
3-4 tablespoons butter
¼ teaspoon fresh thyme, basil, and/or parsley
1 teaspoon lemon juice
3 teaspoons grated Parmesan cheese

Preparation:

1. In 1-quart saucepan over medium heat, melt butter.

2. Add bread crumbs; cook, tossing lightly, until crumbs are golden. Stir in thyme or basil until well mixed.

3. If you like, add lemon juice or a pinch of pepper.

Beef Bourguignon (boor-gee-nyon)

One of France's most famous gastronomic dishes from the Burgundy region.

Ingredients:

3 slices of bacon
1 large white onion, cut up
3 pounds beef for stew, cut into 2-inch chunks
all-purpose flour
1 large carrot
1 large onion
¼ cup brandy
3 garlic cloves, crushed
2 teaspoons salt
½ teaspoon pepper
1 bay leaf
3 cups Burgundy or other good red wine
1 pound mushrooms, sliced
water

Preparation:

1. In 6-quart Dutch oven over medium heat, cook bacon until browned. Then remove bacon.

2. In drippings in Dutch oven, cook onions until lightly brown and slightly caramelized, stirring occasionally. Remove the onions and place in small bowl; set aside.

3. Meanwhile, on waxed paper, coat meat chunks with 3 tablespoons flour. In drippings in Dutch oven over medium heat, cook meat several pieces at a time, until well browned on all sides.

4. In Dutch oven, add the chopped carrots and onion and cook over medium heat, stirring frequently until tender, about 5 minutes.

Pour brandy over all. Add reserved bacon, garlic, salt, thyme leaves, pepper, bay leaf and burgundy. Cover and bake in 325° oven 3½ hours or until fork tender.

5. Meanwhile, in small bowl with spoon, mix ¼ cup water and 4 tablespoons flour until smooth.

6. In Dutch oven, add flour mixture into hot liquid. Blend well. Cover and bake until fork tender. Serve immediately.

Basic Crepes (krehps)

Ingredients:

1 cup flour
1 cup milk
3 eggs, beaten
pinch salt

Preparation:

Whisk all ingredients together till smooth. Put one tablespoon butter into crepe pan over medium heat to coat pan. Pour scant ¼ cup batter into crepe pan. Tip to coat bottom of pan and cook 2 minutes till top is set (underside just brown). With spatula, lift edge of crepe all around, shake pan gently so crepe will come loose. Flip over; cook for 1 minute or until light brown. Slip crepe onto Silpat-lined cookie sheet, keep warm in oven, repeat.

Crepes Suzette (krehps soo zeht)

Suzette Sauce Ingredients:

⅓ cup orange juice
¼ cup butter
2 tablespoons sugar
¼ teaspoon grated orange peal
¼ cup Grand Marnier or other orange flavored liqueur

Preparation:

Put orange juice, butter, sugar, and orange peel in 10-inch skillet over low heat until blended and melted.

Serving the crepes:

Fold crepes in quarters, arrange in sauce in pan. Simmer 5 minutes. Pour the liqueur in center of pan over the crepes. Heat this for 1 minute. Then light with a long match, let liqueur flame until it goes out. Serve immediately!

Spinach Crepes (krehps)

Ingredients:

2 10-ounce packages frozen chopped spinach
¼ cup butter
1 small onion, finely diced
¼ cup all-purpose flour
1 teaspoon salt
⅛ teaspoon pepper
2 cups half & half
1 cup shredded cheese (Monterey Jack, Colby, or any mild-flavored cheese that you like)
crepes from basic crepe recipe

Preparation:

In 2-quart saucepan, cook the spinach as directed on package and drain thoroughly. Meanwhile, in 3-quart saucepan over low heat, melt butter; sauté onions, then stir in flour, salt, and pepper until blended. Over medium heat, gradually stir in half & half. Cook, stirring constantly until thickened. Add cooked spinach and cheese, stirring constantly until cheese melts. Spoon ¼ cup spinach and cheese mixture into center of each crepe and roll up.

Serve warm.

Cheese Blintzes

These freeze well. Freeze before baking; to serve after being frozen, let thaw completely, then bake in buttered baking pan same as in the recipe.

Ingredients:

8 ounces creamed cottage cheese
1 3-ounce package cream cheese, softened
¼ cup sugar
½ teaspoon vanilla extract
2 tablespoons butter
crepes from basic crepe recipe

Preparation:

In small bowl with a mixer at medium speed, beat cottage cheese, cream cheese, sugar, and vanilla until smooth. Spread about 2 tablespoons in each crepe, fold into square packages.

Melt butter in 13 by 9-inch baking pan in oven at 350°F. Remove from oven. Arrange blintzes in one layer in pan. Bake 10 minutes until heated through.

Serving suggestions:

Serve topped with strawberry sauce. (See opposite page.)
I freeze these and then take them camping. It always surprises and delights our friends.

Strawberry Sauce

You can use fresh or frozen berries. You could even try blueberries or raspberries for a change of flavor.

Ingredients:

1 10-ounce package frozen strawberries, thawed
¼ cup water
⅛ cup cornstarch
½ cup sugar

Preparation:

Put thawed strawberries, sugar and water in small saucepan. Make a slurry with cornstarch and small amount of water, add this to the saucepan and heat till the sauce thickens. Keep warm until time to serve.

Truffle Brownies (truhf-fuhl)

Too good for words. Give them a try. You'll love 'em!

Ingredients:

For the batter:
3 tablespoons unsalted butter, plus more for coating the pan
3 ounces good quality unsweetened chocolate, coarsely chopped
½ cup all-purpose flour
¼ teaspoon baking powder
½ teaspoon salt
1 cup sugar
2 large eggs
¼ cup milk
1 teaspoon pure vanilla

For the topping:
4 ounces good quality semisweet chocolate, coarsely chopped
⅔ cup heavy cream

Preparation:

Preheat oven to 325°F. Butter 9-inch springform pan and set aside.

To prepare the batter, put the butter and chocolate in heatproof medium bowl and set over a pan of simmering water. Stir until melted and then remove from heat and allow to cool completely.

Whisk together flour, baking powder and salt in separate bowl. set aside. Put sugar and eggs in a bowl and whip with electric mixer on medium until pale and fluffy. Add chocolate mixture, milk, and vanilla and beat until combined. Add flour mixture, remember to stop the mixer a few times and scrape down the sides to make sure that all the ingredients become incorporated into the batter. Pour the batter into the prepared pan and bake for 27 to 30 minutes. Remove from oven and allow to cool completely in the pan.

To prepare the topping put the chocolate in a medium bowl. Heat the cream in small saucepan until just simmering. Pour the warm cream over the chocolate and let it stand for 1 minute. Then gently stir until smooth.

Pour the topping over the cooled brownies in the pan and let set for about 20 minutes in the refrigerator. Then let stand at room temperature for another 30 minutes. Cut into wedges, wiping knife with a hot, damp cloth between each cut and enjoy.

Chocolate Fondue

You could try a flavored brandy for a change of pace.

Ingredients:

8 ounces dark chocolate
¾ cup heavy cream
2 tablespoons brandy (optional)

Preparation:

Break chocolate into small pieces in small sauce pan together with the heavy cream. Heat the mixture gently, stirring constantly, until the chocolate has melted and blended with the cream. Remove from heat and stir in brandy. Pour into fondue pot or small flameproof dish over a small burner. Serve with a selection of fruit, marshmallows, cookies, etc. for dipping.

Notes

Chapter 4
Chef Suzette's
Italian
Favorites

©Lisa Redington

Bagna Cauda Dip (Bahn-yah Kow-dah)

My mother and I used to frequent a restaurant in Calistoga, California. The bagna cauda dip was creamy and good. The baby vegetables were fresh from the garden.

Ingredients:

2 cups heavy cream
3 tablespoons butter
1 garlic clove, minced
2-ounce can anchovy fillets, drained and mashed
½ teaspoon salt
⅛ teaspoon pepper
1 teaspoon thyme leaves
1 teaspoon oregano leaves

Preparation:

In a 2-quart saucepan over medium heat, bring the cream to a boil, then reduce heat to a simmer and continue until cream is reduced to about 1½ cups. Remove from heat. In a 1-quart saucepan over medium heat melt the butter, cook garlic for 1 minute. Stir in the next 5 ingredients and cook, stirring until smooth. Remove from heat. With wire whisk, gradually whip in the cream and whip until smooth.

Serving suggestions:

Serve with assorted crisp fresh vegetables and breadsticks.

Crostini with Tomato-Basil Topping
(Kroh-stee-nee)

Meaning "little toast" in Italian, with my favorite topping.

Ingredients:

1 baguette (bahg-eht)

A French bread formed into a long narrow cylindrical loaf, crisp on the outside and a light chewy interior. Slice into $1/8$-inch slices. Brush with olive oil (extra virgin) and toast.

The topping has similar ingredients to those in a popular Italian salad (Insalata Caprese); it's considered patriotic in Italy, as its three main ingredients are the colors of the national flag.

Topping Ingredients:

½ pound Mozzarella (optional)
2 large ripe tomatoes
10 fresh basil leaves
¼ cup extra virgin olive oil
pinch of salt

Preparation:

Chiffonade the basil leaves. (Layer leaves one on top of another, roll up lengthwise, and slice thin to make small strips.) Slice mozzarella into tiny (about pea size) squares. Slice tomatoes in half, squeeze out seeds, then slice into squares about the same size as the mozzarella. Add basil and olive oil and salt. Mix well, chill. Serve on Crostini.

Minestrone (mih-neh-stroh-nee)

This hearty stew or soup can be made using many different cuts of beef but my favorite is oxtails.

Ingredients:

1 to 2 pounds ox tails
3 tablespoons olive oil
1 large onion
2 large carrots
2 stalks celery
3 medium potatoes, diced
½ pound green beans, cut into 1-inch pieces
6 cups water
½ small head cabbage shredded
1 16-ounce can diced tomatoes or fresh tomatoes
½ 10-ounce bag fresh spinach coarsely torn
2 medium zucchini, diced
6 beef bouillon cubes
1 teaspoon salt
1 16-ounce can of kidney beans, drained
½ cup grated parmesan cheese

Preparation:

1. In 8-quart Dutch oven or large saucepot over medium heat, in hot oil, cook oxtails until they are are well browned. Add water and simmer oxtails for approximately 2 hours till tender and meat starts to fall off the bone. Add more water if needed.

2. Add onion, carrots, celery, potatoes, and green beans and cook about 20 minutes, stirring occasionally.

3. Add kidney beans, cabbage, tomatoes with their liquid, spinach, zucchini, bouillon cubes and salt. Over low heat, cook for about 20 minutes.

4. Ladle soup into bowls and pass cheese separately to sprinkle over each individual serving.

Pesto (peh-stoh)

I make pesto in big batches every summer and store it in small jars in the freezer to use all winter long.

Ingredients

1 bunch fresh basil, washed
olive oil as needed
3-5 cloves garlic
½ cup pine nuts
½ cup parmigiano-reggiano

Preparation:

Using a food processor, add the basil, garlic, pine nuts and cheese. Start with ⅓ cup olive oil and process. Add olive oil till you reach the consistency wanted.

Serving suggestion:

Toss with favorite cooked noodles.

Use as a rub on baked chicken.

Optional:

Add cooked vegetables, such as zucchini (zoo-kee-nee), carrots, broccoli, etc. when serving on pasta.

Fettuccini Alfredo (feht-tuh-chee-nee al-fray-do)

I have had so many versions of this dish. This is quite simply the best.

Ingredients:

½ stick butter (¼ cup)
¾ cup parmesan cheese, grated
1¼ cup heavy cream
1 package fettuccini noodles
black pepper
fresh garlic, finely minced (optional)

Preparation:

In small 2-quart sauce pan, melt the butter. Add the cream. Sprinkle the cheese in while stirring gently. Season with pepper.

Boil fettuccini till al denté.* Drain noodles, then toss with sauce. Sprinkle with the minced garlic if desired.

———

*Pasta cooked only until it offers a slight resistance when bitten into, but which is not soft or overdone.

Chicken Cacciatore (catch-a-toh-reh)

Classic Italian comfort food. I love the dish served over egg noodles.

Ingredients:

1 tablespoon salad oil
1 3- to 3½-pound chicken, cut up
1 16-ounce can diced tomatoes
½ cup Chianti or other good dry red wine
2 teaspoons garlic, minced
¾ teaspoons basil
¼ teaspoon pepper
12 small white onions or 2 medium onions, peeled and diced
1 large green and 1 large red or orange bell pepper, cut into ½-inch
    strips
1 tablespoon cornstarch
1 tablespoon water

Preparation:

1. In a skillet over medium heat, in hot salad oil, cook the chicken pieces until well browned on all sides.

2. Stir in tomatoes with all their liquid, wine, garlic, basil, and pepper; heat to boiling. Reduce heat to low; cover and simmer 15 minutes.

3. Add onions and green and red/orange peppers; cover and simmer 15 minutes longer or just until vegetables are fork tender.

4. In a cup, stir cornstarch and water until smooth; gradually stir into chicken mixture and cook, stirring frequently, until mixture is boiling and thickened and chicken is fork tender.

Saltimbocca (sal-tim-boh-ca)

Finding an Italian restaurant that has saltimbocca on the menu could prove to be pretty tricky. So now you can make it yourself. It's a very elegant dish for special occasions.

Ingredients:

4 veal cutlets, each cut about ¼ inch thick (optional: Substitute
    chicken breasts for veal.)
¼ cup butter
¼ cup medium sherry
¼ pound thinly sliced prosciutto, cut into thin strips
½ pound provolone or mozzarella

Preparation:

1. Preheat oven to 350°F. With meat mallet, pound cutlets until about ⅛-inch thick, turning once. In 12-inch skillet over medium heat, in hot butter, cook cutlets until lightly browned on both sides. Place in 12 by 8-inch baking dish.

2. To drippings in skillet. add sherry and stir to loosen brown bits; pour over meat. arrange prosciutto strips over veal. Bake 5 minutes. Remove from oven; coarsely shred cheese and sprinkle over cutlets, bake 4 to 5 minutes more till cheese is melted.

Clam Linguine (lihn-gwee-nee)

This is one of those great emergency 10-minute meals. Where everything is out of the pantry and onto the table in a jiffy, but it's oh so good.

Ingredients:

1 16-ounce package of linguine noodles, cooked al denté*
1 6-ounce can clams or fresh clams, minced or chopped
1 teaspoon lemon juice
¼ cup olive oil
2 tablespoons butter
1 teaspoon chopped parsley
1 teaspoon crushed garlic
¼ cup white wine

Preparation:

Sauté all ingredients except pasta together and serve over linguine. Goes great with French bread and a green garden salad.

———

*Pasta cooked only until it offers a slight resistance when bitten into, but which is not soft or overdone.

Chicken Piccata (pih-kah-tuh)

Originally made with veal, but made with chicken it's also good, and less expensive.

Ingredients:

2 pounds chicken cutlets, each cut about ¼ inch thick
salt and pepper
⅓ cup all-purpose flour
¼ cup olive oil
2 tablespoons butter
2 tablespoons capers
1 cup water
½ cup dry white wine
1 chicken flavor bouillon cube or envelope
2 medium lemons
parsley sprigs

Preparation:

1. With meat mallet, pound cutlets to ⅛ inch thickness on waxed paper, sprinkle with 1 teaspoon salt and ¼ teaspoon pepper; coat with flour.
2. In 12-inch skillet over medium heat, in hot olive oil and butter, cook chicken a few pieces at a time until lightly browned on both sides, removing pieces as they brown and adding more oil if necessary.
3. Reduce heat to low. Into drippings in skillet, stir water, wine, bouillon and ½ teaspoon salt, scraping to loosen brown bits. Return chicken to skillet; cover and simmer 15 minutes until cutlets are fork tender. Cut lemon in half; squeeze one half to remove juice; thinly slice the other half. Overlap cooked cutlets on large platter; keep warm. Stir lemon juice into liquid in skillet and add capers. Over high heat, heat to boiling. Spoon liquid over cutlets; garnish with lemon slices and parsley.

Eggplant Parmigiana (pahr-muh-zhah-nuh)

If serving children, peel eggplant first.

Ingredients:

olive oil
2 garlic cloves
1 large onion, chopped
2 16-ounce cans tomatoes
½ teaspoon basil
½ teaspoon salt
1 cup dried bread crumbs
2 eggs
2 tablespoons water
1 large eggplant, cut into ½ inch slices
½ cup grated parmesan cheese
1 8-ounce package mozzarella cheese cut into ¼ inch slices

Preparation:

1. In 9-inch skillet over medium heat, heat 2 tablespoons oil. Cook garlic and onion until tender, then add next 3 ingredients. Reduce heat; cook covered 30 minutes.
2. On waxed paper, place bread crumbs; in small dish with fork, beat eggs and water. Dip eggplant slices in egg then in bread crumbs. Repeat twice to coat slices.
3. Grease 13 by 9-inch baking dish. In 12-inch skillet over medium heat, in 2 tablespoons hot oil, cook a few eggplant slices at a time till golden brown. Add more oil as needed.
4. Preheat oven to 350°F. Arrange ½ eggplant slices in baking dish; cover with ½ tomato mixture; sprinkle with ½ parmesan; top with ½ mozzarella. Repeat. Bake 25 minutes.

Manicotti Noodles (Man-ih-kaht-tee) (Crepe style)

This is a very special old-fashioned recipe. It's melt-in-your-mouth good!

Ingredients:

1 cup flour (all purpose)
4 eggs
1 tablespoon vegetable oil
1 teaspoon salt
1 cup water

Preparation:

Whisk all ingredients together until smooth. Put one teaspoon vegetable oil into crepe pan. Pour ¼ cup batter into crepe pan. Tip to coat bottom of pan and cook 2 minutes until top is set (underside just brown). Use a spatula to lift all around the edge of the crepe. Shake pan gently so crepe will come loose. Flip crepe over and cook for 1 minute or until light brown.

Slip crepe onto a Silpat-lined or parchment-lined cookie sheet. Keep warm in oven; repeat with remaining batter.

Manicotti Filling (Man-ih-kaht-tee)

Ingredients:

2 cups ricotta cheese
2 tablespoons grated parmesan cheese
¾ teaspoons salt
¼ teaspoon pepper
2 eggs
1 8-ounce package mozzarella (shredded)

Preparation:

In medium bowl, mix ricotta cheese, parmesan cheese, salt, pepper, and eggs until well blended.

To assemble the manicotti:

Spoon ⅓ of hot Bolognese meat sauce* evenly into a 15½ by 10½-inch roasting pan. Spoon a heaping tablespoon of cheese mixture down the center of each crepe; top with some shredded mozzarella. Fold crepe edges over cheese. Arrange filled crepes, seam side down, in the roasting pan. Spoon remaining sauce over crepe noodles. Bake 30 minutes until hot and bubbly.

———

*See following page.

Bolognese (boh-loh-nyeh-seh)

Sometimes I add a little red wine, the same wine that I might be drinking

Ingredients:

1 pound lean hamburger
1 medium onion, small dice
1 small red bell pepper, small dice
8-10 mushrooms, sliced
½ cup black olives, sliced
1 or 2 cans tomato sauce
2 cans tomato paste
1 bay leaf
1 tablespoon oregano
½ tablespoon rosemary
1 tablespoon basil
1 package spaghetti or penne noodles
1 cup good red wine (optional)

Preparation:

In 4-6 quart sauce pan, fry the hamburger until no longer pink. Drain off the grease. Add the onion and pepper. Cook for 5 minutes. Add the olives, mushrooms, tomato sauce, paste, herbs, and (optional) wine. Simmer for approximately 1½ hours.

In a separate 8-quart stockpot, boil the pasta in salted water until al denté.* Serve sauce over the noodles.

---

*Pasta cooked only until it offers a slight resistance when bitten into, but which is not soft or overdone.

Zabaglione (zab-bahl-yoh-nay)

A foamy, frothy, light, custard-like dessert. Also known as sabayon or sabayon sauce.

Ingredients:

3 egg yolks
3 tablespoons sugar
3 tablespoons marsala wine
fresh fruit (optional)
pound cake or angel food cake

Preparation:

In a double boiler, bring about 2 inches of water to a simmer. In the top of the double boiler (off the heat), combine the yolks, sugar and wine. Beat with a whisk until well blended. Place over the simmering water and whisk constantly until the mixture is pale yellow and fluffy, about 5 minutes.

Serve immediately over fresh berries and cake.

Yield: 4 servings

Notes

Chapter 5
Chef Suzette's

Chinese
Favorites

©Lisa Redington

Pot Stickers

Yum! Make your own; they're fun and easy.

Filling Ingredients:

¼ lb. ground pork (or chicken or shrimp)
½ cup cabbage, shredded and chopped
¹/₈ cup green onions, chopped fine
1 tablespoon soy sauce
½ tablespoon dry white wine
½ can water chestnuts
½ tablespoon salt
½ teaspoon cornstarch
dash of pepper

gyoza wraps*
¹/₃ cup chicken stock
2 tablespoons vegetable or peanut oil
soy sauce, vinegar and chili oil* for condiments

Preparation:

Mix ingredients for filling in bowl. Place a teaspoon of mixture in center of Gyoza skin. Moisten sides with water and fold in half. Gently press sides together to stick.

To pan fry: Heat 2 tablespoons of oil. Add gyoza, side by side upright to fill pan. Cook over medium heat until bottoms are golden brown. pour in ¹/₃ cup chicken stock and immediately cover pan tightly. Lower flame and cook until all stock has been absorbed. Serve while hot with soy sauce, vinegar and chili oil on the side.

Yield: Makes approximately 25 gyoza.

———

*Found in your local grocery store.

Shrimp Fried Rice

In place of shrimp, you could use crab, scallops, garlic, pork, barbecued pork, chicken, or even tofu.

Ingredients:

3 to 4 cups cooked rice
1½ tablespoons oil (peanut or vegetable)
3 scallions
1 egg (slightly beaten)
1 to 2 teaspoons soy sauce
⅛ cup water chestnuts, minced
4 tablespoons carrot, minced
⅛ cup frozen peas
¼ pound shrimp, cleaned, deveined, and chopped

Preparation:

In a well-seasoned frying pan, over medium heat, stir shrimp with oil till hot. Add carrot, then rice. Don't stir or flip too much; allow to crisp up. Push the rice to one side of the pan. Put the egg on the other side and stir to cook, then stir it all together. Add the rest of the ingredients except soy sauce. Cook for about 3 to 5 minutes, then sprinkle soy sauce all over.

Chinese Chicken Salad

If a Chinese chicken salad doesn't have the fried rice noodles, snow peas, or peanuts, it might be good, but this recipe is great!

Ingredients:

1 small head romaine or iceberg lettuce, torn up
2 cups cooked chicken (baked, broiled, grilled, or boiled), diced
    into bite size pieces
1 bunch scallions, diced
1½ to 2 cups snow peas, blanched and chilled
½ cup roasted peanuts, chopped
1 package rice noodles (Fry approximately ½ package.)
2 teaspoons sesame seeds for garnish
tomatoes for garnish
cilantro for garnish

Preparation:

In a deep pot, fill ⅓ of the way up with vegetable oil or shortening.
Heat up to 375°F.
Fry rice noodles just till they blossom out, remove and drain.
Beware: Noodles grow to about 8 times their size.
Combine all ingredients together, toss with soy vinegar dressing, top
with fried noodles and garnish with tomatoes and cilantro.
Serve with: extra soy vinegar dressing:

Dressing Ingredients:

1½ teaspoons sugar
3 tablespoons soy sauce
3 tablespoons rice vinegar (not seasoned)
1 teaspoon sesame oil
2 tablespoons peanut oil

Preparation:

Combine sugar, soy, and vinegar. Gradually whisk in oils to blend.

Wonton

The choice of filling is yours. They're all so good. Wonton soup is a fantastic dish to serve guests on a cold winter's day.

Filling Ingredients:

2 to 2½ cups cooked meat
½ to 1 cup minced vegetables (carrots, zucchini, etc.—your choice)
1 scallion, minced
1 tablespoon soy sauce
½ teaspoon salt
chicken stock
1 to 2 packages wonton wrappers

Preparation:

Mince or shred meat and vegetables and add soy sauce and salt. Let this mixture stand for about 30 minutes.

Variations for meat: use any of the following combinations:

pork (lean or roast) and shrimp
pork (lean or roast) and crabmeat
pork (lean or roast) and fish fillet
pork (lean or roast) and lobster
chicken, alone or with any of the seafood above

Wonton Wrap and Recipe Techniques

1. Hold the wonton skin in palm of your hand with lower corner pointing toward you.

2. Place about ½ to 1 teaspoon of filling slightly below the center of skin.

3. Moisten the adjacent edges of the skin with water. Fold wonton skin diagonally in half to form a triangle.

4. Press the edges to seal, while at the same time gently pressing out any air pockets, around the filling.

5. Brush a bit of the water on the front of the triangle's right corner and on the underside or back left corner.

6. With a twisting action bring the two moistened surfaces together and pinch to seal. Let dry for 5 minutes

Serving Suggestions:

For wonton soup:

2 quarts chicken broth, preferably homemade, boiling gently

Drop wontons in. Cook for approximately 6 minutes. They will go from opaque to translucent. Garnish with sliced green onions.

Other options:

Fry wontons in vegetable oil till golden brown.

Wontons also freeze well.

Lo Mein with Beef

The term Lo Mein translates to mixed noodles. So be sure to mix well to distribute all the wonderful flavors together

Ingredients:

½ pound fresh Chinese noodles* (lo mein)
3 large dried shiitake mushrooms*
¼ pound flank steak
1 to 2 tablespoons oyster sauce*
¼ teaspoon pepper
2½ teaspoons sesame oil*
peanut, vegetable, or canola oil
½ cup water chestnuts
½ cup any kind of cabbage, cut crosswise shreds. Salt to taste
½ cup chicken broth
½ cup chives cut into 2 inch lengths (optional)
3 cups bean sprouts, rinsed and drained (optional)

Preparation:

1. Drop the noodles into large quantity of boiling water and cook 3½ to 5 minutes, until tender. Do not overcook. Drain, rinse well under cold water. Set aside

2. Place the mushrooms in a bowl and add boiling water to cover. Let stand 15 to 30 minutes or longer, then drain and squeeze them to extract most of their moisture. Cut off and discard tough stems, then slice.

3. Place the meat on a flat surface and cut it across the grain into the thinnest possible slices. Place the slices in a bowl with the oyster sauce, pepper and 1 teaspoon of sesame oil.

4. In a wok or skillet, heat 2 tablespoons of oil to medium-high heat, add beef and cook, stirring constantly, about 1 minute.

5. Add the water chestnuts and mushrooms and cook, stirring, over medium-high heat, about 15 seconds. Add the cabbage and salt. Cook, stirring, about 1 minute.

6. Add the noodles. Cook, stirring, about 20 seconds. Add the soy sauce. Cook about 15 seconds, stirring, and add the chicken broth. Cook, stirring, about 2 minutes, then add the chives and bean spouts, if used. Cook, stirring, 2 minutes more.

7. Add the remaining sesame oil, toss to blend, and serve hot.

———————

* Can be found in Asian markets

Beef and Broccoli in Oyster Sauce

You can also use snow peas or asparagus.

Ingredients:

1 pound beef (The better the cut the better the dish), sliced into bite-size pieces.
1 large bunch of broccoli, cleaned and cut into 1 to 2 inch pieces
1 small onion, sliced
2 tablespoon oil (peanut or vegetable)
1/4 cup beef stock
fresh ginger, 1 thin slice or to taste
3 scallions
1 clove garlic
3 tablespoons or more oyster sauce
2 tablespoons soy sauce
1 teaspoon sugar
1½ tablespoons sherry

Preparation:

In seasoned frying pan or wok, start oil over medium heat. Fry beef till edges are crispy, add broccoli and onion, cook for 2 minutes, then add the rest of the ingredients. Cook until broccoli is tender. If you want to thicken sauce, mix 1 teaspoon corn starch with 3 tablespoons water and add at the same time as the broccoli and onion.

Moo Goo Gai Pan

This dish sounds exotic and hard to prepare, but it's not.

Ingredients:

1 large chicken breast, skinned and boned
5 teaspoons cornstarch
1 teaspoon plus 2 tablespoons water
salt to taste
1 teaspoon dry sherry
¼ teaspoon ground white pepper
1 pound button mushrooms
1¼ cup chicken broth
¼ cup peanut, vegetable, or canola oil
⅓ cup sliced water chestnuts
⅓ cup celery, cut into 2-inch lengths
½ teaspoon sugar
1 15-ounce can straw mushrooms
½ cup walnut halves

Preparation:

1. Cut chicken into the thinnest possible slices. Put the slices into a mixing bowl and add 1 teaspoon of cornstarch blended with 1 teaspoon of the water, salt, sherry, and pepper. Blend to coat the chicken pieces.

2. Cut stems off and rinse button mushrooms. Add to chicken broth. Cover and simmer 5 minutes. Drain and reserve liquid.

3. In wok or skillet heat oil over high heat. Add the sliced chicken. Cook, stirring, just to separate the pieces and until the meat has lost the pink color, about 15 seconds. Drain chicken and set aside, leaving 2 tablespoons of oil in the pan.

4. To the oil in the pan, add the mushrooms, water chestnuts, walnuts, and celery. Cook, stirring, about 2 minutes. Add 1 cup of chicken broth and bring to a rapid boil. Add the sugar, cook about 30 seconds.

5. Blend the remaining cornstarch with water and stir in. When thickened, add chicken. Cook, stirring, until the chicken is piping hot; then it is ready to serve!

Sweet and Sour Pork

Growing up, we ordered various different dishes family style in Chinese restaurants, but we always had to order sweet and sour pork, as it was my father's favorite. And he thinks this is the best recipe he's ever tasted.

Ingredients:

1 pound pork (loin or fillet) cut into 1-inch cubes
1 tablespoon soy sauce
1 egg white
¾ cup cornstarch
2 cups oil for deep frying
½ red pepper plus
½ green or yellow pepper, cut into 1-inch cubes
1 or 2 large carrots cut into ¼ inch diagonal slices
1 can pineapple chunks (reserve liquid)

sauce:

1 cup reserved pineapple liquid, if needed add water
¼ cup sugar
¼ cup white vinegar
¼ cup tomato ketchup
2 tablespoons cornstarch, dissolved in ¼ cup water

Preparation:

1. Lightly pound each piece of pork. Mix with soy sauce, egg white, and cornstarch until evenly coated and well dredged.

2. Heat oil to 400°F in wok. Drop in pork a few pieces at a time. Deep fry three times, 2 minutes each time, removing meat from wok and bringing oil to temperature between each frying. Fry until crispy and golden brown. Drain. Remove. Set aside.

3. Reheat 2 tablespoons of oil in wok to 350°F. Stir-fry red and green/yellow peppers and carrots. Remove.

4. Combine pineapple liquid, sugar, vinegar, and ketchup in saucepan. Bring to boil. Stir constantly. Thicken with dissolved cornstarch.

5. Add peppers, carrots and pineapple to sauce.

6. Put fried pork on platter. Pour sauce over fried pork.

Kung Pao Chicken

Spicy, hot, and really good!

Ingredients:

2 whole chicken breasts, boned, skinned. Cut in to ½-inch cubes
2 tablespoons oil (peanut or veg)
1 small onion
4 stalks celery, slicing ¼-inch diagonally
5 whole dried red chili peppers, or to taste
3 scallions
2 cloves garlic, minced
½ cup skinless roasted peanuts

Sauce Ingredients:

Mix all together:
1 teaspoon chili paste w/garlic
2 tablespoons soy sauce (dark works well)
1 tablespoon sherry
¼ cup chicken stock
1 teaspoon cornstarch
1 teaspoon sesame seed oil

Preparation:

In a large well-seasoned skillet, add oil till hot, over medium heat. Add chicken & onion. Cook till chicken is about half cooked, then add the rest of the ingredients except peanuts. Sauté for about five minutes. Then add peanuts and cook for one more minute.

Notes

Chapter 6
Chef Suzette's

Favorites From India

Poori (poor-ee)

Poori is very popular in northern India as well as neighboring Pakistan.

Ingredients:

1 cup all-purpose flour
1 cup whole wheat flour
1 teaspoon salt
½ cup water
salad oil

Preparation:

1. In medium bowl, stir flours, salt, water and 1½ teaspoons salad oil until roughly blended. (The mixture will be very dry.)

2. In bowl, knead dough until it holds together and is smooth, about 10 minutes. Shape into a ball; place in greased bowl, turning to grease top. Cover with plastic wrap; let rest 10 minutes.

3. Meanwhile, in medium-size skillet, heat 1 inch salad oil to 400°F. With hands, shape dough into 20 balls. On lightly floured surface with lightly floured rolling pin, roll each ball into paper thin circle, 4 inches in diameter. (Edges will be ragged.) Keep remaining dough and finished circles covered with plastic wrap to keep them from drying out.

4. Drop circles, one at a time, into hot oil. With back of slotted spoon, gently hold circle under surface of oil until it puffs up, about 10 seconds. Fry about 20 seconds more, turning once. With slotted spoon, remove poori to paper towels; drain. Serve warm or store and reheat to serve later.

5. To reheat: preheat oven to 325°F. Wrap poori in foil in one layer; heat 5 minutes. (They will be flat.)

Mulligatawny Soup (muhl-ih-guh-taw-nee)

This soup is rich in meat and spices. A wonderful hearty meal.

Ingredients:

5 bacon slices, diced
1½ pounds boneless chicken
4 cups chicken broth
2 carrots, sliced
2 stalks celery, chopped
1 apple, chopped
1 tablespoon curry power
6 peppercorns, crushed
2 whole cloves
1 bay leaf
3 tablespoons all-purpose flour
⅓ cup water
1 cup half and half or coconut milk
1½ cups hot cooked rice

Preparation:

1. In 5-quart Dutch oven over medium heat, fry bacon until crisp. Cut up chicken into serving pieces; add the chicken portions to pan and brown well on each side.

2. Remove chicken pieces and bacon from pan. Drain on paper towels. Pour off any fat in pan.

3. Return chicken and bacon to pan; add the next 8 ingredients. Heat mixture just to boiling.

4. Cover; simmer over low heat 30 minutes, or until the chicken is fork tender.

5. In cup with spoon, blend flour and water.

6. Gradually add flour mixture to simmering soup, stirring. Add half and half; do not boil.

7. To serve: ladle soup into bowls. Spoon a mound of hot rice into each of the bowls.

Chicken and Vegetable Curry

This is how easy making a curry dish can be.

Ingredients:

1 pound boneless chicken meat, cooked and cubed
1 medium red and yellow bell pepper, diced to 1 inch
1 medium onion, chopped
½ cup chicken broth
2 large carrots, sliced
1 tablespoon cumin
2 tablespoons curry powder
3 zucchini, in halved slices
salt and pepper
2 tablespoons vegetable oil
2 cups heavy whipping cream

Preparation:

1. In a large pot or Dutch oven, sauté onions and bell peppers in vegetable oil till tender.

2. Add carrots and cook for 3 to 4 minutes on medium heat till carrots are slightly carmelized.

3. Then add the rest of the ingredients except the cream and cook on low for 30 to 40 minutes, allowing for the spices to blossom.

4. Stir in the cream and cook on medium low for 10 more minutes. Enjoy on rice!

Top off with condiments:

chopped roasted peanuts
shredded coconut
golden raisins
chutney (Try the apple, peach and apricot recipe on page 89.)

Shrimp Curry

I also serve shrimp curry as an appetizer.

Ingredients:

1½ pounds cleaned, shelled and deveined large shrimp
1 medium red bell pepper, chopped into 1-inch squares
1 medium onion, chopped
½ cup chicken broth
½ tablespoon cumin
2 tablespoons curry powder
salt and pepper
2 tablespoons vegetable oil
2 cups coconut milk

Preparation:

1. In a large pot or Dutch oven, sauté onions and bell peppers in vegetable oil till tender.

2. Then add the rest of the ingredients except the coconut milk and shrimp. Cook on low for 30 to 40 minutes, allowing for the spices to blossom.

4. Stir in the coconut milk and shrimp and cook on low for 10 more minutes. Enjoy on rice!

Top off with condiments:

chopped roasted peanuts
shredded coconut
golden raisins
chutney (Try the apple, peach and apricot recipe on page 89.)

Vegetable Pullao

This exotic dish is time consuming but worth it. Mung beans are not well known, oddly enough, because it's what common bean sprouts are.

Ingredients:

1 cup whole mung beans,* picked over and washed
2 cups long grain rice
4½ tablespoons vegetable oil
1 teaspoon whole black mustard seeds*
1 medium-sized onion, peeled and finely chopped
1 large carrot, finely chopped
4 medium-sized cloves garlic, peeled and finely minced
1 teaspoon peeled, finely minced fresh ginger
⅓ pound string beans, trimmed and cut into ¼-inch pieces
¼ pound medium-sized mushrooms, diced
2 teaspoons garam masala*
1½ teaspoons ground coriander
1½ teaspoons salt
2 tablespoons finely minced parsley

Preparation:

Put mung beans in a bowl with 3 cups of water. Cover lightly and set aside for 12 hours. Drain beans and wrap in damp towel. Put the wrapped bundle in a bowl. Put this bowl in a dark place for 24 hours.

Wash rice well and soak in 4 cups of water for half an hour. Drain well.

Preheat oven to 350°F

Heat oil in a wide, heavy 5-quart ovenproof pot over medium heat. When hot, put in the mustard seeds. As soon as they start to pop, add the onion and carrots. Cook for about 5 minutes, stirring, until edges are brown. Add the garlic and ginger. Fry, stirring, for about 1 minute. Turn heat to medium-low and add the mung beans, rice, string beans, mushrooms, garam masala, ground coriander, and salt. Stir and sauté for 10 minutes or until rice turns translucent and vegetables are well coated with oil. Add 4 cups hot water and the minced parsley. Turn heat to medium-high heat and cook, stirring for about 5 minutes or until almost all water is absorbed. Cover the pot first with aluminum foil, and then cover with its own lid. Place in oven for half an hour. Fluff up with a fork.

---

*Found in Asian markets or specialty stores.

Apple, Peach, and Apricot Chutney

Ingredients:

4 ounces dried peaches, quartered
4 ounces dried apricots, quartered
2 ounces golden raisins
4 ounces dried papaya, diced
6 cloves garlic
2 one-inch cubes fresh ginger, peeled and grated
8 fluid ounces white wine vinegar
8 ounces sugar
2 teaspoons salt
½ teaspoon curry powder
4 ounces maraschino cherries

Preparation:

Combine all the ingredients except cherries in a heavy stainless steel pan. Over a medium heat, cook at a vigorous simmer for about 30 minutes or until a thick, jam-like consistency. Add cherries and stir in gently. Let cool. It will thicken more as it cools.

Yogurt with Zucchini

This is a wonderful dish served warm or cold, and another way to use zucchini

Ingredients:

2 medium zucchinis, peeled and grated
salt
1 medium onion, cut lengthwise into half-moon shapes
1½ cups plain yogurt
3 tablespoons vegetable oil
1 teaspoon whole mustard seeds
⅛ teaspoon black pepper
⅛ teaspoon cayenne pepper

Preparation:

1. Place grated zucchini in a bowl and sprinkle with salt. Toss and set aside for 20 minutes. Drain the zucchini and press out the liquid as much as you can.

2. Place yogurt in another bowl. Beat lightly with a whisk until smooth.

3. Heat the oil in an 8-inch skillet over medium heat. When hot, put in mustard seeds. As soon as the mustard seeds began to pop (it takes just a few seconds), put in onions. Stir and fry for about 2 minutes or until the slices are translucent.

4. Add the zucchini. Stir and fry another 3 minutes. Turn off the heat and let zucchini cool slightly.

5. When cooled, fold it into the yogurt. Add ¼ teaspoon salt and pepper and cayenne. To eat warm, place combination in a double boiler on low heat and stir until warm, or eat cold.

Yogurt with Cucumber and Mint

This condiment is used on so many dishes in India, like ketchup is here!

Ingredients:

2 cups plain yogurt
1 cucumber, peeled and cut into ¾ inch dice
2 tablespoons finely minced fresh mint
¾ teaspoon salt
1 teaspoon ground roasted cumin seeds
¼ teaspoon cayenne pepper (optional)
freshly ground black pepper
garnish: 1 small sprig mint

Preparation:

Put the yogurt in a bowl. Beat lightly with a fork or whisk until smooth and creamy. Add the cucumber, mint, salt, ½ teaspoon of the cumin, $^1/_8$ teaspoon cayenne, and a little black pepper. Mix. Empty into a serving bowl. Sprinkle the remaining cumin, cayenne, and some more black pepper over the top. Place the mint sprig in the center.

Khari Poori (poor-ee)

Savory, deep fried cookies with peppercorns, generally eaten as a snack. They can be eaten plain or with sweet chutneys.

Ingredients:

1 cup finely ground whole wheat flour
1 cup unbleached white flour
1 teaspoon salt
1 tablespoon coarsely crushed black pepper
3½ tablespoons vegetable oil,
plus oil for deep frying
water

Preparation:

Sift the whole wheat flour, white flour, and salt into a bowl. Add the black pepper and oil into flour with fingers until the flour resembles coarse oatmeal. Now slowly add very hot water - about ½ cup plus 3 tablespoons - and begin to gather the flour together. Squeeze the dough into a ball. It should just about hold. Do not knead.

Break the dough into about 50 balls. Keep them covered with a plastic wrap.

Heat about 2 inches of oil in any utensil for deep frying over medium heat. While oil is heating, begin to roll out the dough balls until they are about 2 inches in diameter. Fry each for 2-3 minutes or until poori is lightly brown on both sides and crisp, remove and drain on paper towels. Store in airtight container. Keeps for about a week.

Chapter 7
Chef Suzette's
Philippine
Favorites

© Lisa Pedrazan

Fresh Lumpia

This is a delicious and very healthy recipe!

Ingredients

2 tablespoons vegetable oil
3 garlic cloves, pressed
1 small onion, diced
1 medium carrot, diced
2 cups boneless chicken or pork, cut into cubes
or medium sized shrimp, cleaned and deveined
1 can garbanzo beans, drained
½ medium head cabbage, sliced thin and ½ inch long
1 head romaine lettuce, with about 15 to 20 large leaves

Preparation

After removing large lettuce leaves from the head, shred the
remaining little lettuce leaves. Set aside.

In large frying pan, sauté garlic and onions in vegetable oil. Add
meat choice and sauté for 3 to 5 minutes or half cooked. Add carrots
and sauté till tender. Add garbanzos and cabbage, stirring well,
picking up the flavor on bottom of pan. Cook until cabbage begins
to wilt. Place a handful of shredded lettuce into each large romaine
leaf and top with 3 to 4 heaping tablespoons of lumpia. Drizzle on
brown sauce. Recipe follows on opposite page.

Sweet and Sour Brown Sauce

Ingredients

¼ cup water
1 tablespoon cornstarch
2 tablespoons soy sauce
1 tablespoon brown sugar
pinch salt
garlic to taste, freshly chopped

Preparation

Cook all ingredients on medium heat till smooth. Adjust ingredients according to taste. Add garlic to top off dish.

Adobo

The citizens of the Philippines consider this their national dish. It is made up of braised chicken or pork. In the Lujion Province they add coconut milk and peppers. This is my most favorite Filipino dish!

Ingredients

1 pound chicken or pork
½ cup soy sauce
⅛ cup vinegar
3 garlic cloves smashed
8 to 10 whole peppercorns
1 tablespoon vegetable oil
1 to 1½ cups water

Preparation

1. Brown chicken or pork in Dutch oven with vegetable oil, then drain if needed.

2. Add soy sauce, vinegar, garlic, peppercorns and water; simmer till chicken is tender. Add water if needed. It should be very saucy.

Optional: Add 1 can coconut milk and 3 dried Thai peppers; both recipes are wonderful, the coconut adds another level of flavor, and peppers a nice heat.

Tinola

A simple dish anyone can make, but delicious. When the ginger is added an intoxicating aroma will fill the house.

Ingredients

1½ - 2 pounds skinless-boneless chicken thighs
1 tablespoon vegetable oil
1 tablespoon fresh garlic, minced
1 medium onion, chopped up
1 tablespoon fresh ginger, grated
or ¼ cup fresh baby ginger,* sliced thin
3 cups chicken broth
1½ teaspoon coarse-ground black peppercorns
1½ pounds butternut or acorn squash or 3 chayote† (chi-oh-tay)
    cut into 1-inch squares
¼ cup green onions sliced

Preparation

1. Cook chicken thighs in vegetable oil on medium heat till a little browned.

2. Add onions, garlic, ginger, pepper, chicken broth, and squash; simmer till squash is tender.

3. Serve with rice, top with green onions.

———

* Available in Asian markets or gourmet stores.

† Chayote is a fruit the size and shape of a pear, found in most markets or gourmet stores.

Sinigang (sin-a-gong)

My favorite ingredient is the sea bass. It's delicious, and good for you too!

Ingredients

¾ to 1 pound sea bass, shrimp or pork
1 package tamarind soup base*†
3 turnips or taro roots, cut into large chunks
1 bunch turnip greens or spinach, washed and chopped
1 handful of fresh green beans, washed
3 to 4 Japanese eggplant, cut into chunks
6 okra, cut into chunks or left whole if small
3 wax peppers
1 liter water

Preparation

1. Put pork or other choice in pot with the one liter of water; boil, then skim surface if needed.

2. Add tamarind soup base and turnips and cook till turnips are tender. Add remaining ingredients and simmer for 20 to 30 minutes. Serve with rice. Use patis* (fish sauce condiment), sprinkled on as you would soy sauce.

———

* Can be found in Asian markets

† you can substitute ⅛ cup lemon juice for tamarind soup base.

Punsit

Similar to the Chinese chow mein, but with a flavor of its own!

Ingredients

1 package soba noodles,* boiled and drained
1 small onion, diced
3 stalk celery, sliced
2 cloves garlic
1 pound chicken thighs or breasts, cut into 1-inch chunks (Bones
   add flavor, but remove before serving.)
4 cups cabbage, diced
1 tablespoon vegetable oil

Preparation

1. In a Dutch oven, brown chicken chunks and cook onions until tender.

2. Add celery; cook till tender.

3. Add cabbage and garlic; mix well, bringing up the fond from the bottom of the pan for more flavor.

4. Toss in cooked noodles. Mix together well. Serve over rice with patis* (fish sauce condiment), sprinkled on as you would soy sauce.

———————

* Can be found in Asian markets.

Mechado

*There is something familiar yet unusual about this dish. It's
kind of like a stew, but with more pizzazz.*

Ingredients

1 whole chicken, approximately 3 pounds, cut up
or 2 to 3 pounds stew beef or spare ribs
2 big onions, quartered
4 large potatoes, quartered
2 cans tomato sauce
½ cup vinegar
1 red and 1 green bell pepper, cut into large chunks
2 to 3 bay laurel leaves
salt and pepper to taste
2 cups bouillon (chicken or beef)
2 tablespoons soy sauce

Preparation

Brown meat in large stew pot, then add the tomato sauce, vinegar,
bay leaves, soy sauce and salt and pepper. Simmer on low heat for
about an hour, stirring occasionally. Then add onions, peppers, and
potatoes. Continue cooking for 20 minutes or until potatoes are
tender. Serve with rice.

Optional, serve with a little dish of fish sauce (patis)* to sprinkle on
Mechado.

———

*Available at specialty grocery stores.

Poly Tao

We used to grate the coconut fresh for this dessert.

Ingredients

1 cup sweet rice flour*
1/3 cup water

Preparation

Mix ingredients together and make small balls. In a quart pan half full with boiling water, drop some balls in. Wait until they float; this means they're done. Repeat till all balls are cooked. Then roll in coating mixture (below); let cool, and enjoy.

Coating Ingredients:

½ cup grated coconut
¼ cup roasted sesame seeds
1 cup sugar

Preparation:

Mix all together.

———————

* Available in Asian markets or gourmet stores.

Rice Cake

Rice cake is a sweet gooey good confection. Sweet rice is a wonderful product. Give it a try!

Ingredients

2 cups sweet rice* (must use sweet rice)
2 8-ounce cans or 2 cups coconut milk
½ cup brown sugar

Preparation

1. Wash, then cook rice with coconut milk and brown sugar in sauce pan; bring to a boil, turn down to a slow simmer till tender, stirring often.

2. Pour into a 13- x 9- x 2-inch pan. Let cool.

3. Cover with brown sugar and put under the broiler or torch till crispy. The sugar turns into a crunchy caramel topping.

———

* Available in Asian markets or gourmet stores.

Her Next Book...

Suzette's Regional Favorites

Cooking Alaskan Style

Includes such tantalizing dishes as:

• Curried Halibut Puffs with Candied Mango Chutney

• Blackened Shrimp with Chipotle Aioli

• Halibut Timbales with Razor Clam Stuffing

• Smoked Salmon and Dill Savory Cheesecake

• Crab Enchiladas with Green Chile Sauce

• Roast Moose with a Lowbush Cranberry Glaze

• Grilled Fish Tacos with Blueberry Salsa

Notes

Order Form

I would like to order my own or another copy of the book *Suzette's International Cooking* by Suzette Lord Weldon. Please send me:

books x $16.95 per copy =

+ Postage (first class) & Handling @ $4.95/book: _____

_____

TOTAL ENCLOSED $

_____

We accept cash, check, or money order made out to Northbooks, or VISA, Mastercard. Prices subject to change without notice.

(You may phone your VISA/MC order to Northbooks at 907-696-8973)

VISA/MC card # ⬜⬜⬜⬜ ⬜⬜⬜⬜ ⬜⬜⬜⬜ ⬜⬜⬜⬜

Exp. Date: ___ / ___   Amount Charged: $ _____

Signature: _____

Phone Number: _____

Please send my book (s) to:

Name: _____

Address: _____

City: _____ State: _____ Zip: _____

Fill out this order form and send to:

Northbooks
17050 N. Eagle River Loop Rd, #3
Eagle River, AK 99577-7804
(907) 696-8973
www.northbooks.com

Printed in the United States
200057BV00005B/1-261/A

9 780978 976637